Jeffrey Deroine

Ioway Translator, Frontier Diplomat

Greg Olson

Truman State University Press
Kirksville, Missouri

Copyright © 2015 Truman State University Press, Kirksville, Missouri, 63501
All rights reserved
tsup.truman.edu

Cover art: Jeffrey Deroine, detail from George Catlin, *Ioways in London*, engraving, 1844, courtesy Kansas State Historical Society; detail of U.S. Army Corps of Engineers, *Indian Territory...*, 1866, Library of Congress, Maps Division.

Cover design: Teresa Wheeler

Library of Congress Cataloging-in-Publication Data

Olson, Greg, 1959-
 Jeffrey Deroine : Ioway Translator, Frontier Diplomat / Greg Olson.
     pages cm. — (Notable Missourians)
 Audience: Ages 10 to 12.
 Includes bibliographical references and index.
 ISBN 978-1-61248-153-1 (library binding : alkaline paper) — ISBN 978-1-61248-154-8 (e-book)
 1. Deroine, Jeffrey, 1806-1859—Juvenile literature. 2. Missouri–Biography—Juvenile literature. 3. Slaves–Missouri—Biography—Juvenile literature. 4. Free African Americans—Missouri—Biography—Juvenile literature. 5. Fur traders—Missouri River Region—Biography—Juvenile literature. 6. Indian interpreters—United States—Biography—Juvenile literature. 7. Iowa Indians—History—19th century—Juvenile literature. 8. Travelers—Biography—Juvenile literature. 9. Landowners—Missouri—Holt County—Biography—Juvenile literature. I. Title.
 F466.D37O57 2015
 306.3'62092–dc23
 [B]
                                                                   2015012033

No part of this work may be reproduced or transmitted in any format by any means without written permission from the publisher.

The paper in this publication meets or exceeds the minimum requirements of the American National Standard for Information Sciences—Permanence of Paper for Printed Library Materials, ANSI Z39.48–1992.

Contents

Introduction................4

Chapter 1: Life as a Slave.........6

Chapter 2: The Road to Freedom .14

Chapter 3: Life with the Ioways...21

Chapter 4: A Trip to Europe 28

Chapter 5: Back Home in
   Missouri..................36

Legacy: From Slave to World
   Traveler..................44

Timeline.........................45

For Future Reading..............46

Index............................48

Image Credits....................48

Introduction

For the first twenty-six years of his life, Jeffrey Deroine was a slave, but his story is unusual for many reasons. When he was young, he was forced to do hard physical work as a fur trader on the Missouri River, but Jeffrey was also very smart. Although he was not able to read or write, Jeffrey was very good with languages.

While growing up, Jeffrey spoke English and French. And while working for a trader, Jeffrey met and became friendly with many Native Americans and learned five different Native languages. His skill with languages helped Jeffrey gain his freedom.

Jeffrey was one of the few slaves in Missouri who gained his freedom before the Civil War. He filed a lawsuit asking the courts to free him from an owner who mistreated him, but he lost. Later the Ioways, through their agent, arranged to buy Jeffrey from his owner. The Ioways freed Jeffrey and hired him to work as their interpreter. Whenever the U.S. government held a meeting or treaty council with the Ioways, Jeffrey was there to translate.

Jeffrey traveled with the Ioways to such places as New York City and Washington, DC. In 1844 and 1845, he visited Europe with a group of fourteen Ioways, where they performed dances and told stories for the public. The Ioways had the chance to meet famous people and even royalty, with Jeffrey Deroine as their translator.

As a free man, Jeffrey also worked as a trader and a farmer. He was the first African-American known to have owned land in Holt County, Missouri, before the Civil War had even been fought.

Chapter 1
Life as a Slave

When Jeffrey Deroine was born in St. Louis on May 14, 1806, the region around the city was still called the Louisiana Territory. As more settlers moved west of the Mississippi River, the United States broke the huge territory into several smaller ones. In 1812, part of Louisiana became the Missouri Territory. In 1821, Missouri became the twenty-fourth state in the Union.

We don't know who Jeffrey's parents were. His friend Andrew Hughes, Indian agent for the Ioways, said that Jeffrey's father was a French or Spanish fur trader and his mother was a slave. Even though his father was a free white man, Jeffrey was born a slave.

The law classified a person who had any African ancestors as black. Even a person who had one black grandparent and three white grandparents was black in the eyes of the law. In Missouri, and in many other areas in the American South, it was legal for white people to own black people as slaves. In those days, slaves were treated as property just like wagons, houses, and cattle. Because Jeffrey's mother was a slave, as soon as he was born, Jeffrey became the property of the man who owned her.

Jeffrey's first owner may have been a French man named Francis Deroin. Jeffrey lived with Deroin as a child and adopted the family's last name and their Catholic religion. During his lifetime, people

Some slave families were able to live together, or at least live near each other. But slave owners didn't care about keeping families together, and they often sold children away from their mothers, or fathers away from their wives and children.

The Louisiana Territory

The land that makes up the state of Missouri today was not always a part of the United States. France took the region, which they called the Louisiana Territory, from Native Americans in 1682. In 1803, they sold 828,000 square miles of the territory to the United States in a deal known as the Louisiana Purchase. The territory stretched from the Gulf of Mexico to Canada and from the Mississippi River to the Rocky Mountains.

wrote Jeffrey's name many different ways. It appeared in government papers and in letters as Deroin, Dorion, Dorney, and Doraway. The version of his name that appears most often is Deroine (de-rō-NAY).

Traders were some of the first Europeans to come to the Louisiana Territory. Europeans began to bring African slaves to the region nearly a century before Jeffrey was born. The first slaves came from the Caribbean. Once they reached the port of New Orleans, slaves traveled up the Mississippi River to work in lead mines south of St. Louis. Later, settlers from Kentucky and Tennessee moved onto land along the Missouri River. Many of these settlers were farmers who brought slaves with them. These slaves worked as field hands on tobacco and hemp farms.

In May 1804, an expedition led by Meriwether Lewis and William Clark set out to explore the newly acquired Louisiana Territory. The primary goals were to explore and map the new territory, find a route across the continent, and establish an American presence in the area. Secondary goals were to study the geography and the plants and animals, and to establish trade with local Native groups.

Because slaves were property, owners could buy and sell them whenever they wanted. By the time Jeffrey was in his teens, Joseph Robidoux owned him. The Robidoux were a French family of fur traders. Joseph lived in St. Louis, but spent most of his time operating trading posts hundreds of miles away on the Missouri River.

Trading posts were like stores. Robidoux sold things like cooking utensils, guns, ammunition, coffee, sugar, flour, and cloth. Most of his customers were Native Americans who sometimes paid for their goods with money. More often they traded animal hides and furs with Robidoux for the items they needed.

Hunters and trappers often traveled by boat to reach good hunting grounds, then transported their furs by boat to a trading post, where they could exchange their furs for merchandise or for cash.

Europeans liked the hides Native Americans traded to them. They especially liked beaver pelts, which were sent back to Europe and made into felt hats. One large male beaver pelt could be worth a copper kettle, a pair of shoes, or one blanket in trade. Robidoux also traded for deer, elk, and bear hides. These were made into leather goods or fur coats.

Life as Robidoux's slave was not easy for young Jeffrey. As a fur trader, he spent long months away from home. To make it worse, Robidoux was known as a fierce businessman with a bad temper. He once locked a rival trader, Manual Lisa, in a basement to keep him from trading with a group of Pawnee men. Sometimes, if Robidoux was angry with Jeffrey, he would beat him. Once, when Jeffrey was fourteen years old, Robidoux beat him so badly that Jeffrey was afraid Robidoux would kill him.

Skins from elk, antelope, or deer, often called buckskins, were a common unit of trade. A trade good might be described as being worth a certain number of buckskins or "bucks." Today, people often refer to another unit of trade—the dollar—as a "buck."

Fur from beaver pelts could be made into fabric using a process called felting. The felt fabric was formed into hats in various shapes and styles.

Beaver pelts were prized for their warmth and their rich-feeling texture. The pelts were made into coats, or used as trim or lining for clothing.

But the young slave was smart. In those days, the Missouri River was the main travel route for traders from all over the continent, including French traders from Canada and Spanish traders from Mexico and the west, as well as traders from many Native American nations. Robidoux needed to conduct business with all of these people, so Jeffrey learned to speak several languages. He also made friends with many of the people he did business with. He became especially friendly with members of the Ioway nation, who often visited Robidoux's post to trade.

Chapter 2

The Road to Freedom

Jeffrey longed to get away from his owner, Joseph Robidoux. But slaves hoping to make their way to freedom in Missouri had few options. Some slaves tried to run away from their owners, which was very dangerous. There was always a good chance that if Jeffrey tried to run away, Robidoux would catch him and beat him badly again. Owners were never happy to lose slaves. A single slave could be worth more than $1,000 (which is equal to about $23,000 today).

If a slave ran away, his owner would offer a large reward for his return. Some slaves tried to escape to a northern state in the United States where slavery was illegal. Even there, they could be captured by bounty hunters and returned to their masters. For this reason, many tried to leave the United States and reach Canada or Mexico.

A few lucky slaves were able to buy their freedom. Some owners allowed their slaves to do paying jobs for other people, and allowed them to

Abolitionists and free blacks often helped fugitive slaves get to free states where they would be safe. They set up a network of safe houses and people who would hide fugitives from bounty hunters. This informal network was called the Underground Railroad.

15

keep some of the money they earned from this extra work. Even if the slave had to split his wages with his owner, he might be able to save enough money to pay for his freedom. This was very rare. Jeffrey had no way of earning enough money to pay Robidoux. Even if Robidoux had been willing to let Jeffrey buy his freedom, it would have been too expensive.

There was another way slaves could gain their freedom. In 1807, the Louisiana Territory passed a law allowing slaves whose owners treated them badly

In 1826, when Joseph Robidoux was working for the American Fur Company, he founded a trading post at Blacksnake Hills. That trading post later developed into the city of St. Joseph.

In Jeffrey's freedom suit, his grandmother Rachel Camp was called his "next friend." This term was used to describe an adult filing a lawsuit on behalf of a minor in court. Today that person might be referred to as the court-appointed guardian. Jeffrey was only sixteen years old, and as a minor, he was not able to file the lawsuit for himself.

to ask a court of law to set them free. To do this, a slave had to file a lawsuit against his owner. If Jeffrey could prove in court that Robidoux was mistreating him, a judge might make him a free man. In St. Louis, more than three hundred slaves sued for their freedom before the Civil War. But court cases took a long time and they did not always succeed.

Jeffrey thought that asking a court to set him free might work. Because he was not yet an adult, Rachel

Dred Scott

The most famous slaves to sue for freedom were Dred and Harriet Scott. The Scotts sued for freedom because they had once lived in Illinois, which was a free state. Their lawyer told the judge that the Scotts' owner had no right to return them to Missouri and to lives of slavery. The court in St. Louis ruled that the Scotts should go free, but the Missouri Supreme Court said they should remain in slavery. Ten years later, the U.S. Supreme Court in Washington, DC, agreed to hear the case. In 1857, the Supreme Court ruled against the Scotts and they lost their case.

Camp told the court she was his grandmother and filed a lawsuit for him in St. Louis in 1822. They told the court that Robidoux had beaten Jeffrey and was keeping him as a slave against his will. After Jeffrey and Rachel filed their suit, however, nothing happened. Robidoux was an important businessman with many powerful friends and a lot of money. The Indian Agent Andrew Hughes wrote later, "Jeffrey was poor and the Robidoux Company was rich." Robidoux's lawyers used their money and power to keep the case from ever going to trial.

While Jeffrey waited to see if his case would go to trial, he continued to work for Robidoux's trading company. Robidoux operated trading posts along the Missouri River near the present-day site of Omaha, Nebraska, and later at the site of St. Joseph, Missouri. Jeffrey probably had to do such tasks as move heavy crates and casks full of trade goods. Bull boats and steamboats carried goods up and down the Missouri

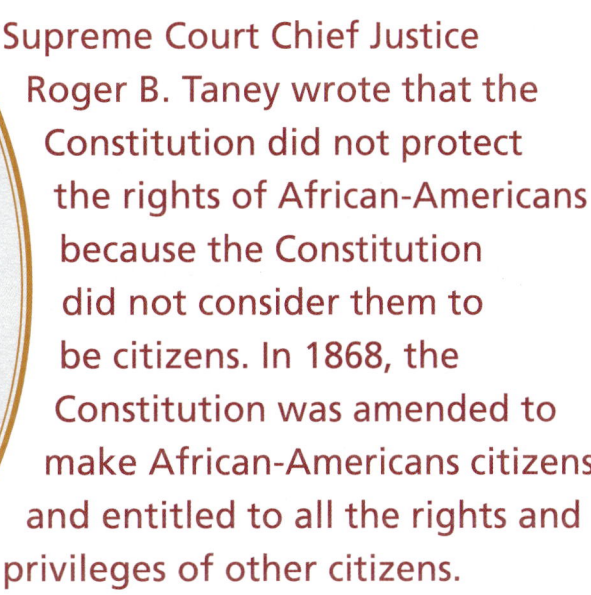

After Dred Scott and his wife, Harriet, lost their Supreme Court case in 1857, they were given to the family of Taylor Blow, who freed them.

Supreme Court Chief Justice Roger B. Taney wrote that the Constitution did not protect the rights of African-Americans because the Constitution did not consider them to be citizens. In 1868, the Constitution was amended to make African-Americans citizens and entitled to all the rights and privileges of other citizens.

19

River between St. Louis and Robidoux's stores. Jeffrey likely helped load and unload ninety-pound packs of animal pelts onto the boats. He would also have had to learn to paddle canoes and bull boats in the river's dangerous currents.

Jeffrey would have also been introduced to a wide variety of colorful characters at the trading post. Robidoux's customers included French traders, American settlers, U.S. military men, and Native Americans from the Ioway, Otoe, Dakota, Osage, Kaw, and Omaha nations.

While working at the post, Jeffrey met two men who would change his life: Francis White Cloud, a leader of the Ioway people, and his friend Andrew Hughes. The U.S. government had assigned Hughes to make sure that the Ioways lived peacefully with other Native nations and nearby settlers.

The Ioways' villages were near Robidoux's post and they often traded with him. While working at the trading post, Jeffrey got to know the two men well. He also learned to speak to Francis White Cloud and to other Ioways in their own language. White Cloud and Hughes grew to like Jeffrey. Together, the two men helped Jeffrey gain his freedom from Joseph Robidoux.

Chapter 3
Life with the Ioways

In July 1830, the Ioways attended a large treaty council at Prairie du Chien, Wisconsin. The U.S. government called at least nine Native American nations to this large meeting. The United States wanted two things. First, the government wanted the Native American nations to promise to live peacefully with each other. Second, it wanted to buy land from the Native Americans because settlers were moving into the region.

The Ioway leaders at the treaty council included Francis White Cloud's father, who was also called

Several treaties were signed at Prairie du Chien, one in 1825, two in 1826, and one in 1830. The fourth Treaty of Prairie du Chien was negotiated between the United States, the Ioway, and other Native groups in the Missouri River Valley.

White Cloud. The elder White Cloud was eager to show the U.S. government that the Ioways were its friends. After several days of speeches, ten Ioway leaders signed what they thought was a treaty of friendship with the United States. Only later did the Ioways learn that the treaty said they had agreed to sell thousands of acres of land in Iowa and Missouri to the U.S. government.

    The Ioways were angry. They told Agent Hughes that they did not speak English well enough to fully understand the treaty they had signed. They told him they would not follow the treaty because they believed they had been tricked. After that, the Ioways realized that it was important to have someone they knew and trusted to translate for them during meetings with government officials.

The Ioways thought Joseph Robidoux's slave, Jeffrey Deroine, could help them. He had been their friend for several years and could speak their language almost as well as they could. They asked Agent Hughes if they could hire Jeffrey as their interpreter. But there was one problem. Jeffrey was still a slave, and the U.S. government refused to hire slaves. Jeffrey could only become the Ioways' interpreter if Robidoux agreed to set him free.

Andrew Hughes asked Robidoux if he would free

White Cloud became a leader of the Ioway people after his father, Wounding Arrow, was killed in battle. White Cloud was one of ten Ioway leaders at the treaty council in Prairie du Chien.

At the 1830 council at Prairie du Chien, William Clark was one of the men who represented the United States government.

THE FIRST DISCUSSION OF THE PLATTE PURCHASE

When Missouri became part of the United States, Native Americans were promised that they could keep land west of the new state. But as American settlers moved west, they began to settle on Native land and wanted the U.S. government to make a new agreement to buy land in what is now northwestern Missouri.

Jeffrey, but the trader was not happy about losing his skilled assistant. Hughes and the Ioways finally made a deal with Robidoux. In March 1832, Robidoux agreed to sell Jeffrey for $600 (which is equal to about $14,000 today). We do not know for sure who bought Jeffrey's freedom. Years later, Francis White Cloud said he had paid for Jeffrey. He probably meant that the Ioways had used some of the tribe's money to pay Robidoux.

The Ioways freed him, so when Jeffrey was twenty-six years old, he became an employee of the U.S. government. He translated for the Ioways whenever they met with their agent or with traders. He also traveled with the Ioways for meetings in cities like St. Louis and New York. Whenever the Ioways held treaty councils with the United States, Jeffrey made sure the Ioways understood the documents they signed.

In 1836, Jeffrey witnessed an important treaty known as the Platte Purchase. In that treaty, the Ioways sold land to the United States that became Holt, Platte, Atchison, Andrew, and Buchanan Counties in Missouri. When Jeffrey signed the treaty as a witness, he made an X on the paper because he had never learned to write his name.

The Ioways were so thankful for Jeffrey's help that in 1838, they asked the government to pay him fifty dollars each year for the rest of his life. The

Treaties

Until the 1860s, the United States considered Native American tribes to be foreign nations. Because of this, government officials had to enter into formal treaties with tribes any time they wanted to settle disputes or buy land. Each of these treaties then had to be ratified by the United States Senate.

government agreed. In 1838, fifty dollars was worth about the same as one thousand dollars today.

But not everyone was happy with the Ioways' interpreter. Some government officials in Washington, DC, thought Jeffrey was too friendly with Francis

A long wooden stem was added to a small stone pipe that was the center of many Native American pipe ceremonies. The pipe might be elaborately carved and decorated. When a person puffs on the pipe, the smoke coming out of his mouth symbolizes truth being spoken, and the plumes of smoke rising upward make a path for prayers to travel to the Great Spirit. Sharing a pipe is considered a sign of friendship and peace.

White Cloud, who became the Ioways' leader after his father died in 1834. These officials told Jeffrey that he was paid only to translate for the Ioways. They warned him not to give the Ioways advice or to help them decide what they should do. Some officials worried that Jeffrey and Francis White Cloud were trying to turn the Ioways against the U.S. government.

The government also accused Jeffrey of selling whiskey to the Ioways. Long before Jeffrey was born, traders had begun using whiskey to cheat Native Americans. The traders discovered that if they could get Natives to drink enough whiskey, the Natives might sell them furs for less than they were worth. Later, traders found that some Native people were so eager to buy alcohol they would trade a large number of pelts just to get it. Whiskey led to violence and it disrupted family life. Because of this, the Ioways and their agent made it illegal for anyone to sell alcohol or drink it on Ioway land.

No one ever proved that Jeffrey sold whiskey or tried to turn the Ioways against the United States. Even so, the government fired Jeffrey from his job as interpreter in 1842.

Chapter 4
A Trip to Europe

Even after Jeffrey Deroine lost his job as the Ioways' interpreter, he remained friends with them, especially with Francis White Cloud. In 1844, White Cloud had the chance to go to Europe. The Ioways' agent allowed him to choose the people he wanted to travel with him. White Cloud selected thirteen Ioway men, women, and children to make the trip. He also asked his friend Jeffrey to go. Francis White Cloud knew Jeffrey would be helpful in Europe because he spoke French as well as English. Jeffrey's former owners, Francis Deroin and Joseph Robidoux, both came from French families and Jeffrey probably spoke both English and French when he was growing up. Many traders had either come directly from France, or had French parents or grandparents.

The Ioways planned to meet their old friend George Catlin in London. Catlin was an artist who painted pictures showing how Native Americans lived. He had first visited the Ioways in 1832 when he traveled on the Missouri River on a steamboat called the *Yellowstone*. On that trip, he made more than one hundred paintings. Some were portraits of the Native people he met along the way. Other paintings showed buffalo hunts, Native villages, and special dances.

George Catlin was an American artist who traveled throughout the American frontier. He painted portraits and made drawings of Plains Indians in their own territory and in Native dress. Catlin traveled to Europe with his "Indian Gallery," and attracted crowds of people fascinated by his view of Natives on the American frontier.

The group of Ioway who visited London and Paris included seven men, four women, and three children.

Many of Catlin's paintings can still be seen in art museums all over the world.

In the early 1840s, Catlin took five hundred of his paintings to England. Europeans were very curious about Native Americans. Catlin knew they would pay to look at his paintings, but he thought they would pay even more to meet real Natives. He asked the Ioways to be a part of a show. He planned to display his pictures in a large gallery. He also planned that each evening, Francis White Cloud and his friends would play music and dance for the audience. Jeffrey would translate as the Ioways told stories and talked about their culture. Catlin believed the show would be very popular and would make money for him and for the Ioways. Because the Ioways were poor and needed money, they agreed to travel to Europe and be part of Catlin's show.

On July 1, 1844, the Ioways sailed from New York aboard a ship named the *Oxford*. They arrived in Liverpool, England, and traveled to London to meet Catlin. After recovering from their long voyage across the sea, they began to perform in the show.

The people of London were thrilled to see the Ioways sing, dance, and, with Jeffrey's help, tell stories. They had heard that all Native Americans were wild savages. For this reason, some English people were afraid to attend the show. They were scared by the way the Ioways looked and by the spears, knives, and war clubs they carried.

They soon realized that the Ioways were happy to be in England and that they were friendly. Many found the Ioways' clothing and their songs and dances to be very exciting. Some women thought the Ioway men were very good looking, and a few returned to watch their performance over and over again.

In addition to his color paintings, Catlin also made drawings and sketches of Native groups, including this one of the group of Ioway who visited Europe in 1844. Jeffrey Deroine is the second person from the right.

Francis White Cloud was in his early twenties when he became the Ioways' leader after his father died. He struggled to do what was best for his people in a world that was changing very quickly.

Jeffrey was also popular in England. Though he did not dance and sing, he shared the stage with the Ioways. If a performer wanted to explain a song or a dance or wanted to tell the audience a story, Jeffrey was there to translate. For this reason, he was the public voice of the Ioways. The popularity of the Ioway shows was partly due to Jeffrey's ability to talk to the audience in a way that captured their attention.

Jeffrey also translated for the Ioways offstage. When they were not performing, the travelers toured European cities and often visited famous people. In England,

Catlinite

Many Native American groups on the Plains use pipes made of red stone called pipestone in their pipe ceremonies. In the 1830s, George Catlin painted pictures of the quarry in Minnesota where the stone for these pipes came from. Since that time, the red stone has been known as catlinite, in his honor. Native Americans still quarry for catlinite at Pipestone National Monument.

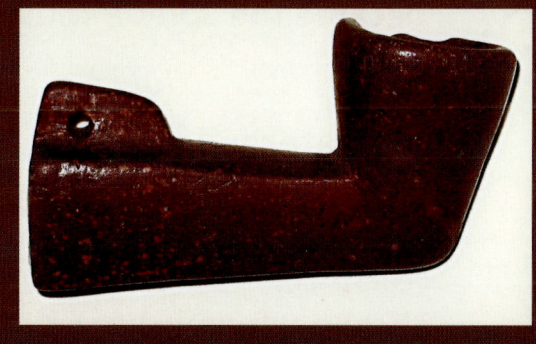

The Tuileries Palace was built in Paris in 1564 and was added to over the centuries until it formed a closed rectangle. King Louis-Philippe I lived there until 1848 when the palace was invaded by revolutionaries. The palace was burned in 1871, but the stone exterior was not damaged. The interior was restored and became the Louvre Museum.

and later when the show moved to France, Jeffrey accompanied the Ioways everywhere they went. When the Ioways visited the Palace of the Tuileries, they performed for King Louis-Philippe I and the royal family of France. The king had been to America and was very interested in Native Americans. He asked

George Sand's real name was Amandine-Aurore-Lucile Dupon. Authors often used a pen name to protect their privacy. Women often chose male pen names because critics were often prejudiced against female writers.

Victor Hugo's novels often dealt with political and social issues of his time. His novels include *The Hunchback of Notre Dame* and *Les Miserables*, both of which tell stories of social injustice. Hugo also wrote poetry and drew.

Jeffrey to tell the Ioways how happy he was that they had visited.

Jeffrey and the Ioways also met members of England's royal family and the famous French writers Victor Hugo and George Sand. Everyone was impressed with Jeffrey's stately manner and his ability to talk with both poor people and noblemen. It was even rumored that at least one woman in the French royal family was captivated by Jeffrey's good looks. It seemed that he was able to impress people wherever he went.

Chapter 5

Back Home in Missouri

After his trip to Europe, Jeffrey worked as a farmer and as a trader. As a free man, Jeffrey Deroine was able to do many things that he had not been able to do while he was a slave. In 1841, the county court in Holt County had given him special permission to buy land there. Slaves were not allowed to own property in Missouri, and before the Civil War, it was rare for free blacks to own property. But Jeffrey had proven himself to be an honorable man and he was allowed to buy a 160-acre farm across the Missouri River from the Ioways' reservation. Land along the river had very rich soil, and many farmers grew corn and hemp to sell.

Jeffrey also continued to work as a trader. As more and more people began passing through St. Joseph on their way to the west, Jeffrey and other traders made money by selling supplies to emigrants stocking up for their long journey.

A ferryboat took people and cargo across the river from Missouri to the Ioways' land. On the Missouri side of the river, the boat landed on Jeffrey's property at a spot known as Jeffries Point.

Jeffrey remained friends with Francis White Cloud and the Ioways, and continued to work for them as a translator. Then some people again accused Jeffrey of selling whiskey to the Ioways. Others said he and Francis White Cloud were stealing some of the annuity

An 1844 map shows Jeffries Point. Later, after William Banks bought Jeffrey's farm, the area became known as Iowa Point.

money that was supposed to be shared with all the Ioways. William Banks, a prominent white farmer from Missouri who knew both Jeffrey and the Ioways, told the government that he did not think Jeffrey was the kind of man who would cheat the Ioways.

Despite the support of Banks and others, in 1846 the U.S. government told Jeffrey he was no longer welcome on the Ioways' land. Francis White Cloud tried to hire him back as an interpreter, but the Ioways' agent would not let him. Even after his removal, Jeffrey continued to collect the annual payment of fifty dollars the Ioways had promised him years before. After Jeffrey settled down to farm his land, he also got married. His first wife was Ioway.

Most white people would not marry someone who was not also white, but in the French territory of Louisiana in the 1700s, it was not uncommon for French traders to marry Native American women. Many times, such marriages were arranged to strengthen business ties. If a trader married the daughter of an important Native leader, he could

Trade

Native Americans once grew or hunted all of their food and made everything they needed to live. After the arrival of European traders, Native Americans began to rely on them for many things they needed, like guns, blankets, and iron kettles. To pay for these things, Natives spent more time hunting for furs to trade and less time hunting to feed themselves. As a result, they sometimes did not have enough food to last through the winter. This made them even more dependent on the traders.

expect that his father-in-law would buy trade goods only from him. The leader would advise other members of the tribe to buy from him as well. At the same time, the leader expected his son-in-law to offer him the best trade goods before he offered them to anyone else.

It was also not unusual for blacks and Native Americans to marry. Because whites discriminated against both, the groups shared a common bond. Some tribes, like the Cherokees, kept blacks as slaves. But other tribes allowed runaway slaves to hide from their masters on tribal land. Some say that escaped slaves hid on the Ioways' land as they made their way to freedom in the north. Some blacks stayed with Native people long enough to marry and become adopted tribal members.

Jeffrey lived and worked closely with the Ioways for much of his life. So it is not surprising that he was married to two Ioway women. His first marriage to Su-See Baskette, who was Francis White Cloud's adopted daughter, was short. They had one daughter, who they named Eliza Jane. Later, Jeffrey married a second Ioway woman. We do not know the name of his second wife, but we know that they had two children: Bela and Jesse.

While Jeffrey was able to marry Native American women, he would never have been able to legally

American settlers began heading west in the 1840s, and many wagon trains passed through the St. Joseph area. In 1845, about 2,700 emigrants headed west looking for good farm land. After gold was discovered in California in 1848, many more people began moving west. In 1850, about 50,000 emigrants traveled to California and Oregon on the Overland Trail.

Slavery ends in Missouri

The Emancipation Proclamation, issued by President Lincoln in January 1861, only freed slaves in Confederate states. Missouri was part of the Union, but still allowed slavery. On January 11, 1865, Missouri approved an ordinance abolishing slavery in the state. This was three weeks before the U.S. Congress proposed an amendment to the Constitution to end slavery throughout the country.

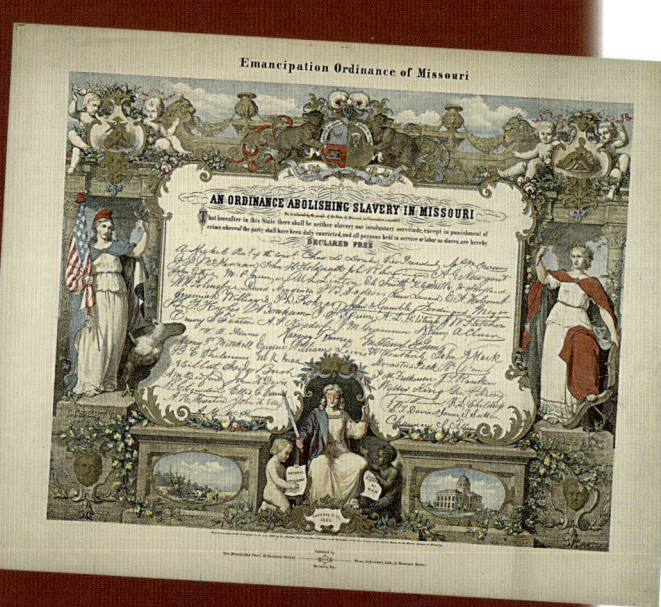

marry a white woman in Missouri. Jeffrey was considered to be African-American, even though his father was European. Laws that forbid blacks from marrying whites were as old as the United States and were meant to keep people of different races separated. Some of these laws existed until the 1960s, more than one hundred years later.

Jeffrey's friend Francis White Cloud died in 1851. At about that same time, Jeffrey married one last time. His third wife had been a slave and was from Kentucky. Jeffrey had been a successful

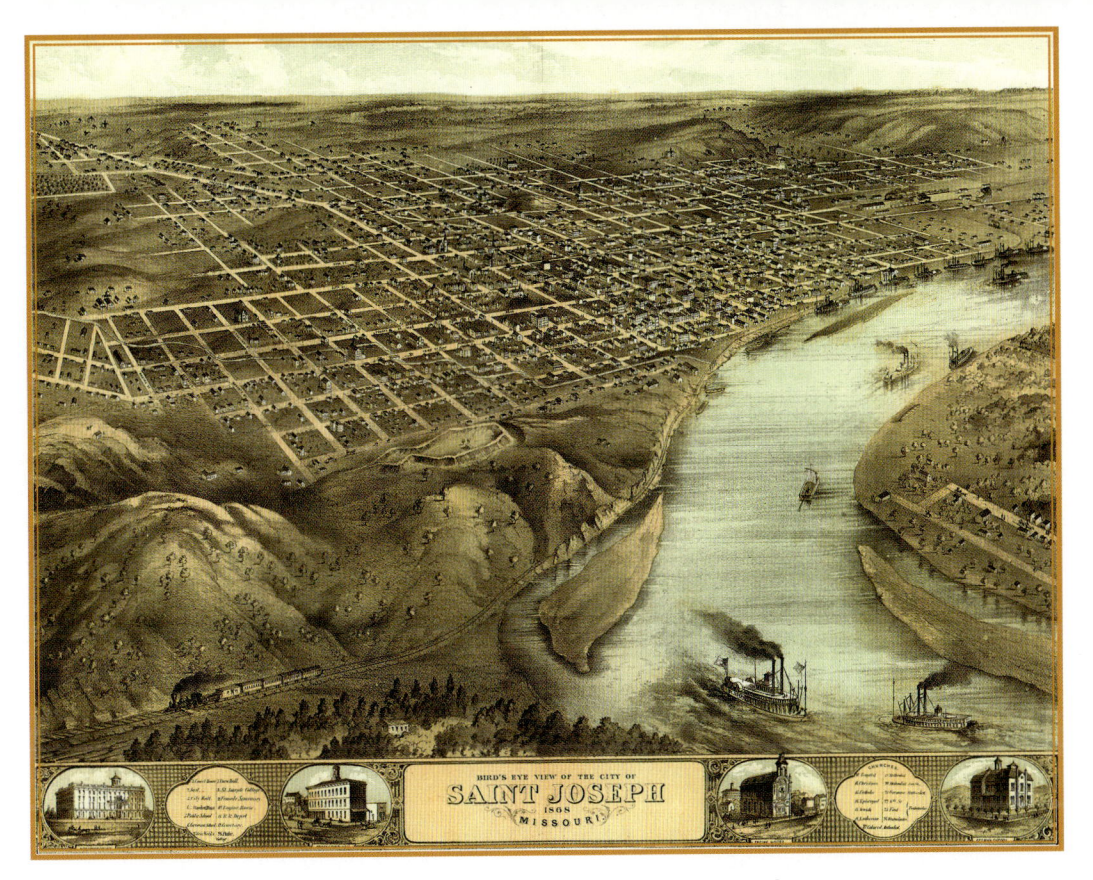

When Jeffrey lived in the St. Joseph area, the town was an important trading center and a starting point for people heading west. In 1860, there were about 9,000 people living in St. Joseph. Today the population is nearly 77,000.

farmer and trader for many years, and he saved enough money to buy her freedom.

Around that time, Jeffrey also sold his farm. William Banks bought Jeffrey's farm and Jeffrey and his wife moved to St. Joseph, where he continued to work as a trader. Jeffrey died there in March 1859, when he was fifty-two years old. It is likely that Jeffrey was buried in St. Joseph. Many years after he died, the Catholic Church moved the cemetery, so no one today knows for sure where he is buried.

Legacy

From Slave to World Traveler

When slavery was legal in the United States, many whites believed that African-Americans were not capable of doing everything white people could do. But Jeffrey Deroine proved those people wrong. Jeffrey learned to speak many languages and served as an interpreter for the Ioway. He was as comfortable speaking to the king of France as he was talking to American settlers and French trappers at a Missouri trading post.

    Jeffrey escaped the bonds of slavery. He also did many things that most Americans of his time, both white and black, did not have a chance to do. He owned land and became a successful farmer and trader. He worked for the government as a translator for the Ioway and was a witness to important treaty talks. He traveled to Europe and met famous people. For a poor boy born into slavery, Jeffrey Deroine had an amazing life.

Timeline

1682: French explorer René-Robert Cavelier, sieur de La Salle, claims all the land along the Mississippi River and all of the rivers that flow into it for France. La Salle and others believe a medieval European law called the Doctrine of Discovery allows them to claim the Native Americans' land.

1782: France gives the part of Louisiana that was west of the Mississippi to Spain in a treaty they keep secret from their British enemies.

1800: Realizing they cannot control the Territory because it is too large and too far from Spain, the Spanish government sells Louisiana back to France.

1803: The United States buys the territory that includes present-day Missouri from France in the Louisiana Purchase.

1806: Jeffrey Deroine is born in St. Louis on May 14.

1807: The Louisiana Territory passes a law allowing slaves who believed their owners were mistreating them to sue for their freedom.

1812: A part of the Louisiana Territory becomes the Missouri Territory.

1821: The Missouri Territory becomes the twenty-fourth state in the Union.

1822: Rachel Camp files a lawsuit in St. Louis Circuit Court on Jeffrey's behalf.

1832: U.S. Indian Agent Andrew Hughes arranges for the Ioways to buy and free Jeffrey from his owner, Joseph Robidoux, so he can work as the Ioways' interpreter.

1836: Jeffrey translates for the Ioway and signs the Platte Purchase treaty.

1838: The Ioways grant Jeffrey Deroine $50 a year for the rest of his life.

1841: Jeffrey buys a 160-acre farm in Holt County, Missouri.

1842: Jeffrey loses his job as the Ioways' interpreter.

1844–1845: Jeffrey and fourteen Ioways travel in Europe with the painter George Catlin.

1846: Superintendent of Indian Affairs Thomas Harvey bans Jeffrey Deroine from the Ioways' Great Nemaha Subagency.

1851: Jeffrey Deroine's friend Francis White Cloud dies at about age 40.

1859: Jeffrey dies in St. Joseph, Missouri, at the age of 52.

1865: The Civil War ends and slavery is abolished.

For Further Reading

Books For Young Readers

Foster, Lance M. *The Indians of Iowa*. Iowa City: University of Iowa Press, 2009.

Kirkpatrick, Jane. *A Name of Her Own*. Colorado Springs: Waterbook Press, 2002. (The story of an Ioway woman named Marie Dorion.)

Mihesuah, Devon A. *American Indians: Stereotypes & Realities*. Atlanta, GA: Clarity Press, Inc., 1996.

Olson, Greg. *Great Walker: Ioway Leader*. Kirksville, MO: Truman State University Press, 2014.

Peterson, Cris. *Birchbark Brigade: A Fur Trade History*. Honesdale, PA: Calkins Creek, 2009.

Sivertson, Howard. *The Illustrated Voyageur: Paintings and Companion Stories*. Duluth, MN: Lake Superior Port Cities, 1999.

Swain, Gwenyth. *Dred and Harriet Scott: A Family's Struggle For Freedom*. St. Paul, MN: Borealis Books, 2004.

Treuer, Anton. *Atlas of Indian Nations*. Washington, DC: National Geographic Society, 2013.

Websites

"The Beaver and Other Pelts." *McGill Library Digital Collections*. http://digital.library.mcgill.ca/nwc/history/01.htm

"Dred Scott." *HistoryNet*. http://www.historynet.com/dred-scott

"The Dred Scott Case." *Jefferson National Expansion Memorial*. http://www.nps.gov/jeff/planyourvisit/dredscott.htm

"The Great Lakes Fur Trade." *The Mitten*. http://seekingmichigan.org/wp-content/uploads/2013/08/Fur-Trade-Mitten.pdf

Ioway Cultural Institute. *Student Resources*. Ioway.nativeweb.org/students.htm.

National Park Service, Jefferson National Expansion Memorial. "Freedom Suits." http://www.nps.gov/jeff/learn/history-culture/freedom-suits.htm

Sources

Blaine, Martha Royce. *The Ioway Indians*. Norman: University of Oklahoma Press, 1995.

Catlin, George. *Adventures of the Ojibbeway and Ioway Indians in England, France, and Belgium*. Vol. 2. 1852, repr., Whitefish, MT: Kessinger Publishing, n.d.

Jeffrie, a mulatto boy v. Robidoux, Joseph, Oct 1822. Case No. 39, Circuit Court Case Files, Office of the Circuit Clerk, City of St. Louis, Missouri. Online at St. Louis Circuit Court Historical Records Project: http://stlcourtrecords.wustl.edu.

Olson, Greg. "Slave, Trader, Interpreter, and World Traveler: The Remarkable Story of Jeffrey Deroine." *Missouri Historical Review* 107 (July 2013): 222–30.

Thorne, Tanis C. *The Many Hands of My Relations: French and Indians on the Lower Missouri*. Columbia: University of Missouri Press, 1996.

Viola, Herman J. *Diplomats in Buckskin: A History of Indian Delegations in Washington City*. Washington, DC: Smithsonian Institution, 1981.

Willoughby, Robert J. *The Brothers Robidoux and the Opening of the American West*. Columbia: University of Missouri Press, 2013.

Index

Catlin, George, 29–31, 32

farmer, Jeffrey as, 36–37, 43

Francis White Cloud, 20, 24, 26–27, 28, 32, 37, 41, 42

freedom suits, 16–18

fur trade and traders, 8, 10–13, 16, 39–40

Hughes, Andrew, 20, 22, 23–24

Ioways, 20, 21–23, 24–27, 37, 39, 40

Ioways, trip to Europe, 28, 31–35

marriage, and Jeffrey, 39–42

pipes and pipestone, 26, 33

Robidoux, Joseph, 10, 11–13, 16, 18–20, 23–24

Scott, Dred, 18, 19

slavery, 6–7, 8, 10, 14–16, 23, 42

trader, Jeffrey as, 11, 13, 18–20, 36, 43

translator, Jeffrey as, 23–27, 31–36, 37

treaties, 21–22, 25, 27,

White Cloud, 21–22, 23

Image Credits

Original art by John Hare: pgs. 6, 14, 21, 28, and 36.

Courtesy of Kansas State Historical Society: cover and p. 4 (detail), and p. 32 (full image), George Catlin, *Ioways in London*, engraving, 1844, W. H. Miner, *The Ioway* (Cedar Rapids IA: Torch Press, 1911).
Library of Congress, Maps Division: cover, detail of U.S. Army Corps of Topographical Engineers, *Indian Territory, with part of the adjoining state of Kansas, etc.* (Washington, DC: Engineer Bureau, War Dept. 1866) (g4021e ct003199); p. 9, *Discovering the Legacy of Lewis and Clark...* (Philadelphia: Lewis and Clark Heritage Foundation, 2003) (g41271 ct001114); p. 39, Karl Bodmer, *Bellvue: Mr. Dougherty's Agency on the Missouri*, 1832–43 (cph 3a10420); p. 42, Emancipation Ordinance of Missouri, E. Knobel and Theodore Shrader (St. Louis: Westliche Press, 1865) (pga 01805); p. 43, A. Ruger, *Bird's Eye View of the City of Saint Joseph, Missouri, 1868* (Merchant's Lithographing Co.) (g4164s pm004370).
Library of Congress, Prints and Photographs Division: p. 7, "A slave father sold away from his family," from *The Child's Anti-Slavery Book...* (New York, 1860) (LC-USZ62-76081); p. 10, Historic American Buildings Survey, Restored interior of William Connor Trading Post, Hamilton County, IL (HABS IND,29-NOBL.V.2-2); p. 15, *In the swamp*, lithograph, 1863 (cph 3g02522); p. 22, J. O. Lewis, *View of the Great Treaty Held at Prairie du Chien, September 1825*, lithograph, 1835 (cph 3b52019); p. 23, C. B. King, *Ma-Has-Kah or White Cloud, an Ioway Chief*, lithograph, 1837 (LC-USZC4-4752); p. 23, reproduction of *Portrait of William Clark* by Charles Wilson Peale (cph 3a52077); p. 34, Charles Fichot, *Paris moderne: Les Tuileries...*, lithograph, 1850 (LC-DIG-ppmsca-31565); p. 37, F. Palmer, *The Ferry Boat*, lithograph, 1847 (pga 04822); p. 41, *Caravan of emigrants for California...*, wood engraving, 1850 (LC-USZC4-2635).
From Wikimedia Commons: p. 12, *Cervus canadensis* (North American elk), photo by James St. John, 2007; p. 12, Dept. of the Interior, *About 150 pelts ...*, Mud Lake NWR, Minnesota, NARA, ARC ID 283846; p. 13, *A felted wool hat reproduction...*, photo by Themightyquill, 2006; p 13, *Beaver lake*, photo by Makedocreative 2011; p. 19, Louise Schultz, *Dred Scott*, 1888, digital image © 1998 Missouri Historical Society, St. Louis; p. 19, Bureau of Printing and Engraving, *Portrait of Roger B. Taney*; p. 26, bottom left, National Park Service, *Craftsman carving a pipe*, Pipestone National Monument; p. 33, Catlinite pipe, probably Ioway, Wamampito Site, Bremer County, Iowa; p. 34, Franz Zaver Winterhalter, *King Louis Philippe*, oil on canvas, 1839; p. 35, Nadar, *Portrait of George Sand*, March 1864; p. 35, Salted paper print of Victor Hugo (retouched), 1853.
Courtesy of Missouri State Archives: p. 17, detail of pages from *Jeffrie, a mulatto v. Joseph Robidoux*, Oct. 1822, Case No. 39, Circuit Court Case Files, Office of the Circuit Clerk. City of St. Louis, Missouri, http://stlcourtrecords.wustl.edu; p. 24, Capital mural of Andrew Hughes; p. 38, map of Missouri, ca. 1844.
Courtesy of State Historical Society of Missouri: p. 16, Portrait of Joseph Robidoux (SHS MO 015226).
Retrieved from Wikimedia Commons: Metropolitan Museum of Art: p. 11, George Caleb Bingham, *Fur Traders Descending the Missouri*, ca. 1845, oil on canvas, Morris K. Jesup Fund, 1933. **Brooklyn Museum:** p. 26 top, Sisseton, Sioux inlaid pipe bowl with two faces, early 19th century, Brooklyn Museum, Henry L. Batterman Fund and the Frank Sherman Benson Fund, 50.67.104; p. 26, bottom right, Native American, Plains, Pipe bowl representing owl, early 20th century, pipestone, Brooklyn Museum, Gift of Cynthia Hazen Polsky, 80.98.2; **National Portrait Gallery:** p. 29, William Fisk, *George Catlin*, oil on canvas, 1849, NPG.70.14. **National Gallery of Art:** p. 30, George Catlin, *Iowa Indians who Visited London and Paris*, 1861/1869, Paul Mellon Collection; p. 32, George Catlin, *The White Cloud, head Chief of the Ioways*, oil on canvas, 1844/45, NGA 1965.16.347.

MN/S/U